GARY

Edwin Smith and David Renouf

APPROACH TO MUSIC

BOOK ONE

Illustrated by Anthony Colbert

Music Department
OXFORD UNIVERSITY PRESS
44 CONDUIT STREET, LONDON W.1

CHAPTER ONE

Making Music with Five Notes

Drum

While the drummer plays these eight bars, the class form into a circle and join hands. (If you belong to a mixed group, each girl should stand on the right of a boy.) The drummer continues the ostinato pattern throughout the dance, varying the dynamics as he thinks fit.

A

Round to the left we go, round and round we go, then, back to the right we go,

B

round and round we go, then, in - to the cen - tre, back to the side a-gain,

A

in - to the cen - tre, back to the side a-gain, Round to the left we go,

round and round we go, then, back to the right we go, round and round we go, then,

C

Take your part - ner round the ring, Prom-en-ade to - geth - er, Take your part-ner

A

round the ring, Prom-en-ade to - geth - er, Round to the left we go,

round and round we go, then, back to the right we go, round and round we go.

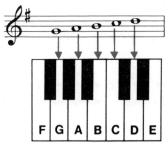

F G A B C D E

3

Say each of the following rhythms twice: leader first, class immediately after. Maintain a steady beat throughout; do not pause between the phrases or stop to correct errors.

Tap with fingers on the chair or desk for quavers. Stamp for crotchets. Nod the head forwards or backwards for rests.

Here are the rhythms of some tunes which employ the same five notes that you have been singing. Can you identify them and say which is which when you hear them played?

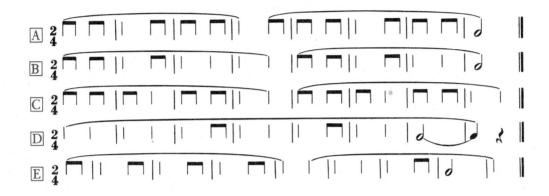

A RUSSIAN FOLK-SONG

This tune is played by flute, oboe, horn, and bassoon. Listen to the performance several times until you can readily distinguish between the four instruments.

NOTES		RESTS (silences)
o	*semibreve, whole note*	—
𝅗𝅥	*minim, half-note*	▬
♩	*crotchet, quarter-note*	𝄽
♪	*quaver, eighth-note*	𝄾
𝅘𝅥𝅯	*semiquaver, sixteenth-note*	𝄿

5

Setting Words to Music

Oboe and flute,
Horn and bassoon,

Hear them together
In a well-known tune.

1. Say the poem and draw a bar-line in front of each syllable that might be stressed. Draw a double bar at the end.

| O - boe and |flute, |Horn   and bas-|soon, |
| Hear them to-|geth-er In a | well - known |tune. ‖

2. Say the poem again and conduct two-in-a-bar. Write $\frac{2}{4}$ at the beginning.

3. Write a note under each syllable.

4. Underline the syllables that need quick notes.

$\frac{2}{4}$ *means* $\overset{2}{}\!\!\downarrow$, *or*

2 crotchets in a bar

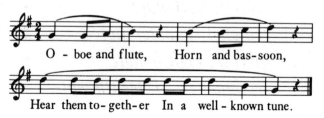

5. Give tails to the notes.

6. Insert rests (silences) where required.

7. Think of a tune, e.g.

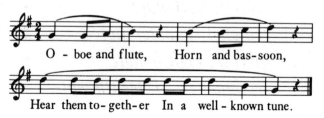

6

8. Write a part for clapping or drumming. This is called a 'rhythmic counterpoint'.

9. Try another tune, e.g.

10. Complete each of the following tunes and rhythmic counterpoints.

11. Now compose a setting entirely your own.

Continue the following rhythmic counterpoints:

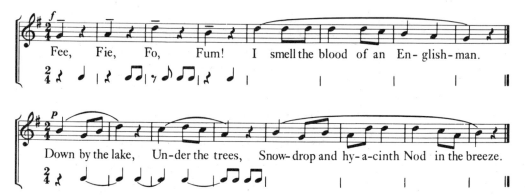

Fee, Fie, Fo, Fum! I smell the blood of an En- glish- man.

Down by the lake, Un- der the trees, Snow- drop and hy- a- cinth Nod in the breeze.

Add a rhythmic counterpoint:

There was an old man of Pe - ru, Who watch'd his

wife a - mak - ing a stew. Once, by mis- take, In a

stove she did bake That un- for- tu - nate man of Pe - ru.

Compose melodies and rhythmic counterpoints for these verses.

> Fox went out in a hungry plight,
> Prayed for the moon to give him light,
> For he'd many a mile to trot that night,
> Before he reach'd his den O!
> (Folk-Song)

> The squalling cat and the squeaking mouse,
> The howling dog by the door of the house,
> The bat that lies in bed at noon,
> All love to be out by the light of the moon.
> (R. L. Stevenson)

LA PETITE ANNA

1 Connaissez vous l'histoire,
Hum, hum, hum, ha, ha, ha;
Connaissez vous l'histoire
De la petite Anna?
Ah, ah, ah, ah,
De la petite Anna?

2 C'était une paresseuse,
Hum, hum, hum, ha, ha, ha;
C'était une paresseuse
Qui ne travaillait pas.
Ah, ah, ah, ah,
Qui ne travaillait pas.

3 C'était une gourmande
Qui goûtait tous les plats.

4 C'était une méchante
Qui battait tous les chats.

5 C'était une menteuse
Qui trompait son papa.

6 Son père qui le sut,
La prit et la fouetta.

7 Elle courut dans le bois,
Mais le loup l'attrapa.

8 Elle voulut se sauver,
Mais le loup la croqua.

9 Tout le monde disait
C'est bien fait pour Anna!

Adopt the following rhythm:

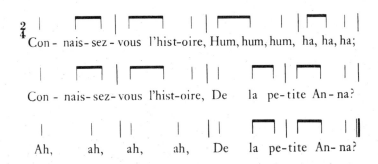

A SAD STORY

1 Do you know the story
Of Little Anna?

2 She was a lazy girl
Who didn't work.

3 She was a glutton
Who relished every dish.

4 She was a naughty girl
Who beat all cats.

5 She was a story-teller
Who deceived her father.

6 Her father, who knew,
Took her and whipped her.

7 She ran away to the wood
But the wolf caught her.

8 She tried to escape
But the wolf gobbled her up.

9 Everyone said
It served Anna right!

Three Rounds for you to Sing

In four parts:

Words anon.

Jen-ny, come tie my, Jen-ny, come tie my, Jen-ny, come tie my bon-ny cra - vat. I've tied it be-hind, I've tied it be-fore, I've tied it so oft-en I'll tie it no more.

An Introduction for 'Jenny, come tie my':

The Tonic Chord of G Major

In three parts:

Music by Cherubini

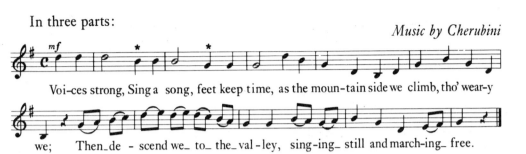

Voi-ces strong, Sing a song, feet keep time, as the moun-tain side we climb, tho' wear-y we; Then de - scend we to the val -ley, sing-ing still and march-ing free.

In two parts:

Words anon.

Andantino

Lit-tle lad, lit -tle lad, Where wast thou born?

Far off in Lan-ca-shire Un - der a thorn.

An Introduction for 'Little Lad':

Smoothly

Recorder 1

Recorder 2

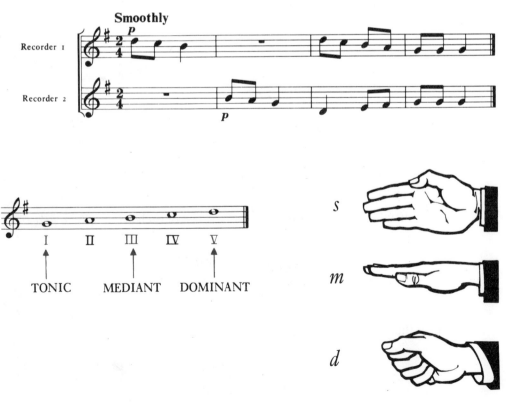

I   II   III   IV   V

TONIC   MEDIANT   DOMINANT

s

m

d

A Little Joke

Here are the five notes we have been using:

 four quavers and a minim

On the piano it is quite easy to play them twice as quickly:

 four semiquavers and a crotchet

or even twice as quickly again:

 four demisemiquavers and a quaver

It is equally easy to play the same patterns on higher or lower notes:

or the left hand might select only the first and last of each group of five notes:

and play them as staccato quavers:

In the following version, the five-note *runs* in the R.H. are answered by *leaps* of a fifth in the L.H.:

Notice, too, that there are also contrasts of
    (i) dynamics—R.H. moderately loud; L.H. quiet
    (ii) phrasing and emphasis—R.H. slurred demisemiquavers and stressed staccato quavers; L.H. light staccato quavers.

Now listen to 'A Little Joke' several times and follow the score during some of the performances.

A LITTLE JOKE by Dmitri Kabalevsky

'A Little Joke' is a most effective *scherzo* based entirely upon '*runs*' of demi-semiquavers and '*leaps*' of quavers.

It is in TERNARY FORM: A B A

In the 'A' music:
    the runs and leaps travel downwards
    the runs come first and appear in
      the R.H.
    the leaps follow the runs and are
      played by the L.H.

In the 'B' music:
    the runs travel upwards
    the leaps travel sometimes upwards
      and sometimes downwards
    the leaps come first in the R.H.
    the runs follow the leaps and are
      played by the L.H.

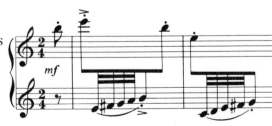

Listen to the music again and then answer these questions by reference to the score.

1. In which bar does the 'B' music commence?
2. In which bar does the 'A' music return?
3. What contrast of dynamics can you find in bars 1 and 2?
4. What contrasts of phrasing are there in bars 1 and 2?
5. Which are the first bars containing a *crescendo*?
6. Which are the first bars containing a *diminuendo*?
7. At the end of bar 8 the notes of the opening of the piece return. What difference is there in the *dynamics*?
8. Is there any difference of *notation* between bars 1–8 and 9–16?
9. Explain carefully what happens in the 'B' music—
   (i) bars 16–20; (ii) bars 20–24; (iii) bars 24–28; (iv) bars 28–32; (v) bars 33–34.
10. Bars 34–42 are the same as bars   ?
11. Write a list of the black notes used in bars 42–53.
12. Listen once again to bars 42–53. Can you guess what is meant by '*senza rit.*'?

Music Workshop

Simple, home-made percussion instruments can be very useful in bringing colour and variety to your rhythmic counterpoints.

COCONUT SHELLS

Saw a coconut in half. File the rims smooth so that the two halves of the shell fit well together.

Make the sound of horses' hooves by clashing the two halves together.

Compose a tune for the following poem and invent a rhythmic counterpoint which will suggest the trotting of the little grey mare when played upon the coconuts.

JOHN COOK'S MARE

1 John Cook he had a little grey mare;
   He haw hum!
   Her back stood up, and her bones they were bare;
   He haw hum!

2 John Cook was riding up Shooter's Bank,
   He haw hum!
   And there his nag did kick and prank;
   He haw hum!

3 John Cook was riding up Shooter's Hill;
   He haw hum!
   His mare fell down and she made her will;
   He haw hum!

4 The saddle and bridle are laid on the shelf;
   He haw hum!
   If you want any more you may sing it yourself!
   He haw hum!

CHAPTER TWO

Contrasting Major and Minor

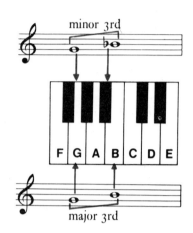

Sing and play the intervals of a
major third and a minor third.

Point out three major thirds and six minor thirds in the following:

Words anon.

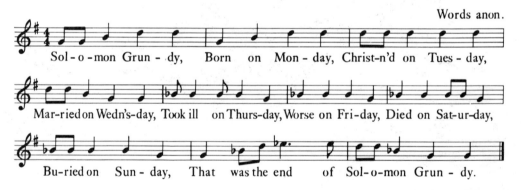

Sol-o-mon Grun - dy, Born on Mon - day, Christ-n'd on Tues-day,

Mar-ried on Wedn's-day, Took ill on Thurs-day, Worse on Fri-day, Died on Sat-ur-day,

Bu-ried on Sun - day, That was the end of Sol-o-mon Grun - dy.

Notice also the effect of the
E flat on the word 'end'—
a minor sixth from G and
a minor second from D.

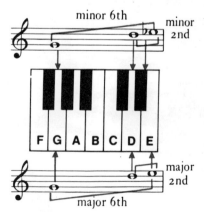

Editing

Since the B flat and E flat are used consistently from bar five to the end, the *mode* has changed from major to minor. We may cancel the F sharp belonging to the key signature of G major:

 ·and substitute the B flat and E flat of the key of G minor:

We can encourage a more effective interpretation of the words and let our minor thirds and minor sixth make their point if:

1 we slow down in the second line and even more in the third
2 we emphasize certain notes by placing *accents* over them
3 we dwell upon the sorrowful 'end' of Solomon Grundy with a *pause*
4 we indicate appropriate *dynamics* (*f* = loud ; *mf* = moderately loud ; *p* = quiet ; *pp* = very quiet ; *ppp* = as quietly as possible ; *crescendo* = growing louder ; *decrescendo* = growing quieter).

SOLOMON GRUNDY

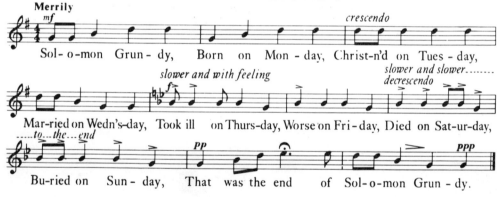

DOTTED NOTES

Can you name these tunes? Copy them out and complete them. Write the words under the notes.

19

Here are two fine tunes, the first in the minor and the second in the major, associated with the British sea song, 'Spanish Ladies'.

SPANISH LADIES

Sturdily

mf

1. Fare-well and a-dieu to you fair Span-ish la-dies,

Fare-well and a-dieu to you la-dies of Spain,

cresc.

For we've re-ceived or-ders to sail for old Eng-land,

ff

But we hope in a short time to see you a-gain.

2 We hove our ship to with the wind at sou'west boys,
   We hove our ship to for to strike soundings clear,
   Then fill'd the main topsail and bore right away boys,
   And straight up the Channel our course we did steer.

3 The first land we made it is called the Dodman,
   Next Rame Head, off Plymouth, Start, Portland and Wight;
   We sailed by Beachy, by Fairly and Dungeness,
   And then bore away to the South Foreland Light.

$\dfrac{3}{4}$ *means* $\dfrac{3}{\text{♩}}$, *or*

3 crotchets in a bar.

11

10

3

Portland

12

2

1

Dodman

Rame Head

Start Point

Scilly Isles

20

The numbers represent the following places: Portsmouth, Dover, Land's End, Plymouth, Cardiff, Southampton, Padstow, Hastings, Exeter, London, Eastbourne, and Bristol. Can you match up the numbers and places?

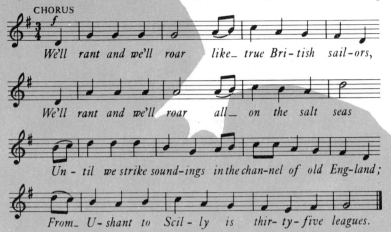

CHORUS

We'll rant and we'll roar like true British sailors,
We'll rant and we'll roar all on the salt seas
Until we strike soundings in the channel of old England;
From Ushant to Scilly is thirty-five leagues.

4 The signal was made for the grand fleet to anchor,
All in the Downs that night for to sleep;
Now stand by your stoppers, see clear your shank painters,
Haul up your clew garnets, stick out tacks and sheets.

5 Now let every man toss off a full bumper,
Now let every man take off his full bowl,
For we will be jolly and drown melancholy,
With a health to each jovial and true-hearted soul.

Here are some poems chosen to give you practice in changing from major to minor.

King David and King Solomon
Led merry, merry lives,
With many, many lady friends
And·many, many wives;
But when old age crept over them,
With many, many qualms,
King Solomon wrote the Proverbs,
And King David wrote the Psalms.

J. B. Naylor

Read through several times and decide upon—
(1) the style (*merry* in the first half; *solemn* in the second)
(2) time signature and bar lines
(3) rhythm (notice how long notes can help to emphasize 'old age crept').
    Begin by allotting one note per syllable. Later you may decide to introduce
    additional notes on certain syllables.

(4) the tune

Editing

(1) Add slurs where there are two notes to a syllable (King)

(2) Add staccato dots to lighten some notes (mer-ry)

(3) Change the key signature from G major to G minor, bar 8

(4) Add indications of mood and dynamics

(5) Include accents > and a pause ⌢ where appropriate

(6) Conclude with a double bar

A LUNATIC'S LOVE SONG

1 O, know you the land where the cheese-tree grows,
And the unicorn spins on the end of his nose;
Where the sea-mew scowls on the circling bat,
And the elephant hunts in an opera hat?

2 'Tis there that I lie with my head in a pond,
And play with a valueless Tichborne bond;
'Tis there that I sip pure Horniman's tea
To the sound of the gong and the howling sea.

3 'Tis there that I revel in soapsuds and rum,
And wait till my creditors choose to come;
'Tis there that I dream of the days when I
Shall soar to the moon through the red-hot sky.

4 Then come, oh come to that happy land!
And don't forget your galvanic band;
We will play at cards in the lion's den,
And go to bed when the clock strikes ten.

Anon.

The change from major to minor might be used in each of the four verses, but not in the same line.
Use the following ideas in the first verse if you wish to—or compose all the music yourself.

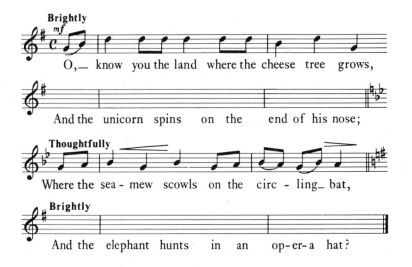

Brightly
mf

O,— know you the land where the cheese tree grows,

And the unicorn spins on the end of his nose;

Thoughtfully

Where the sea - mew scowls on the circ - ling bat,

Brightly

And the elephant hunts in an op-er-a hat?

HOW DOTH THE LITTLE . . .

How doth the little crocodile
  Improve his shining tail,
And pour the waters of the Nile
  On every golden scale!

How cheerfully he seems to grin,
  How neatly spreads his claws,
And welcomes little fishes in,
  With gently smiling jaws!

Lewis Carroll

THE HERRING LOVES

The herring loves the merry moonlight,
  The mackerel loves the wind;
But the oyster loves the dredging song,
  For she comes of a gentle kind.

from THE WALRUS AND THE CARPENTER

'I weep for you', the Walrus said
  'I deeply sympathize.'
With sobs and tears he sorted out
  Those of the largest size,
Holding his pocket-handkerchief
  Before his streaming eyes.

'O Oysters,' said the Carpenter,
  'You've had a pleasant run!
Shall we be trotting home again?'
  But answer came there none—
And this was scarcely odd, because
  They'd eaten every one.

Lewis Carroll

C = *Common Time another form of the Time Signature* $\frac{4}{4}$

THE KEYS OF CANTERBURY

Folk-Song from Somerset

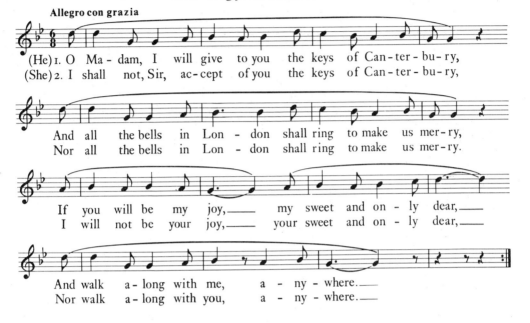

Allegro con grazia

(He) 1. O Ma - dam, I will give to you the keys of Can - ter - bu - ry,
(She) 2. I shall not, Sir, ac - cept of you the keys of Can - ter - bu - ry,

And all the bells in Lon - don shall ring to make us mer - ry,
Nor all the bells in Lon - don shall ring to make us mer - ry.

If you will be my joy,—— my sweet and on - ly dear,——
I will not be your joy,—— your sweet and on - ly dear,——

And walk a - long with me, a - ny - where.——
Nor walk a - long with you, a - ny - where.——

He 3

O madam, I will give to you a pair of boots of cork,
The one was made in London, the other made in York,
If you will be my joy, my sweet and only dear,
    And walk along with me, anywhere.

She 4

I shall not, Sir, accept of you a pair of boots of cork,
Though both were made in London, or both were made in York.
I will not be your joy, your sweet and only dear,
    Nor walk along with you, anywhere.

He 5

O madam, I will give to you a little golden bell,
To ring for all your servants, and make them serve you well,
If you will be my joy, my sweet and only dear,
    And walk along with me, anywhere.

She 6

I shall not, Sir, accept of you a little golden bell,
To ring for all my servants, and make them serve me well.
I will not be your joy, your sweet and only dear,
    Nor walk along with you, anywhere.

He 7

O madam, I will give to you, a gallant silver chest,
With a key of gold and silver, and jewels of the best,
If you will be my joy, my sweet and only dear,
    And walk along with me, anywhere.

She 8

I shall not, Sir, accept of you a gallant silver chest,
A key of gold and silver, nor jewels of the best.
I will not be your joy, your sweet and only dear,
    Nor walk along with you, anywhere.

He 9

O madam, I will give to you a broidered silken gownd,
With nine yards a-drooping and training on the ground,
If you will be my joy, my sweet and only dear,
    And walk along with me, anywhere.

She 10

O Sir, I will accept of you a broidered silken gownd,
With nine yards a-drooping and training on the ground.

Both

Then { I will be your joy, your / you shall be my joy, my } sweet and only dear,
And walk along with { you, / me, } anywhere.

$$\frac{6}{8} = 6 \times \eighthnote$$

$\frac{6}{8}$ = 6 *quavers in a bar*—

The six quavers are grouped into two sets of three.

Unless the music is very slow, we count two in a bar rather than six

$\frac{6}{8}$ is therefore *compounded* of two and three and is known as a COMPOUND TIME as opposed, for example, to $\frac{4}{4}$ which is a SIMPLE TIME.

Here are some well-known $\frac{6}{8}$ rhythms:

O_____ dear_____ what can the mat-ter be?

O, Ma - dam I will give to you the keys of Can - ter-bu-ry.

The Camp-bells are com-in', o-ho, o-ho, The Camp-bells are com-in', o-ho, o-ho.

Can you name some other songs in $\frac{6}{8}$?

Can you whistle these three $\frac{6}{8}$ tunes?

Old English folk-dance tune 'Dargason'

Gaily

Repeat indefinitely End here

Smetana, 'Vltava'

Allegro

Grieg, 'The Cowkeeper's Tune'

Andante con moto

Write down the rhythms usually associated with these words:

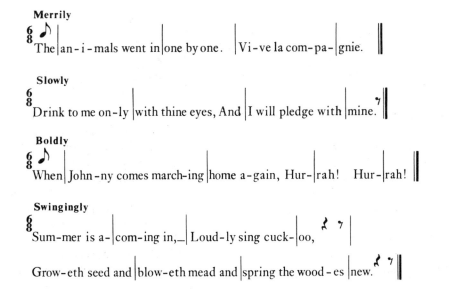

Merrily

$\frac{6}{8}$ | The | an - i - mals went in | one by one. | Vi - ve la com-pa- | gnie. ‖

Slowly

$\frac{6}{8}$ Drink to me on-ly | with thine eyes, And | I will pledge with | mine. ‖

Boldly

$\frac{6}{8}$ When | John - ny comes march-ing | home a-gain, Hur- | rah! Hur- | rah! ‖

Swingingly

$\frac{6}{8}$ Sum-mer is a- | com-ing in,_ | Loud-ly sing cuck- | oo,

Grow-eth seed and | blow-eth mead and | spring the wood - es | new. ‖

27

Nonsense Rhymes

Poems by Edward Lear to set to music in $\frac{6}{8}$ time.

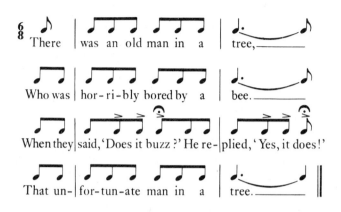

There was an old man in a tree,——
Who was hor-ri-bly bored by a bee.
When they said, 'Does it buzz?' He re-plied, 'Yes, it does!'
That un-for-tun-ate man in a tree.

With a swing

There was an old man in a tree,——
Who was hor-ri-bly bored by a bee.——
When they said, 'Does it buzz?' He re-plied, 'Yes, it does!'
That un-for-tun-ate man in a tree.——

There was a young lady whose bonnet
Came untied when the birds sat upon it.
   But she said, 'I don't care—
   All the birds in the air
Are welcome to sit on my bonnet'.

There was an old man with a beard,
Who said, ''Tis just as I fear'd,
   Two owls and a hen,
   Four larks and a wren,
Have all built their nests in my beard'.

There was a young man of Coblenz,
The length of whose legs was immense.
   He went with one prance
   From Turkey to France—
That remarkable man of Coblenz.

There was an old man on some rocks
Who shut his wife up in a box.
   When she cried, 'Let me out!'
   He exclaimed, 'Without doubt,
You will spend all your life in that box'.

In setting the next poems, we will experiment with changing the *Time Signature* as well as the *Key Signature*.

THE DUCHESS'S LULLABY

Speak roughly to your little boy,
  And beat him when he sneezes,
He only does it to annoy,
  Because he knows it teases.
Baby: Wow! Wow! Wow!

I speak severely to my boy,
  I beat him when he sneezes;
For he can thoroughly enjoy
  The pepper when he pleases!
Baby: Wow! Wow! Wow!

Lewis Carroll

There will be no argument about the style of the first four lines! Sharp staccato accented notes will help to emphasize the aggressive mood and strong syncopations underline the violence of 'beat him' and 'sneezes'.

When we come to the Baby's part, we may either continue in a similar style and let him howl in furious protest or, alternatively, decide upon a contrast. Suppose the Baby is a silly one, quite unmoved by the Duchess's abuse, and we let the music change abruptly from a Malicious March to a Wishy-Washy Waltz.

Syncopation

the effect is that of a syncope, i.e. missing a heart-beat.

Syncopation

a displacement of the musical accent to weak beats or off-beats. In 'beat him' and 'sneezes' the strongest note lies between the 1st and 2nd beats, i.e. it is 'off the beat'.

29

Complete the setting of the first verse and then write in a similar style for the second verse. A strong syncopation suits the explosive 'pepper' just as well as 'beat him' and 'sneezes'. Edit the music carefully.

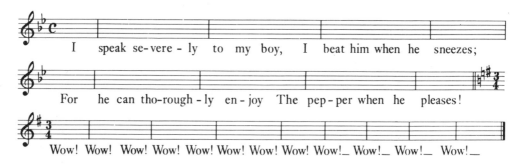

I speak se-vere - ly to my boy, I beat him when he sneezes;

For he can tho-rough - ly en - joy The pep - per when he pleases!

Wow! Wow! Wow! Wow! Wow! Wow! Wow! Wow! Wow!_ Wow!_ Wow!_ Wow!_

Complete this setting of the first verse of 'The Pelican Chorus' by Edward Lear.

Pomposo

King and Queen of the Pe - li - cans we; No other birds so grand as we!

None but we have feet like fins! With lovely leathery throats and chins!

Tempo di Valse

Ploff_skin, Pluff_skin, Pe - li - can jee! We_think no birds so_ hap-py as we!

Plump_skin, Plosh_kin, Pe - li - can Jill! We think so then, and we thought so still!

30

from *POLONAISE IN G MINOR by J. S. Bach*

A ROUND IN G MINOR

Sing in two parts.

The North Wind doth blow, And we shall have snow,
He'll sit in the barn To keep him-self warm,

And what will the ro - bin do then, poor thing?
And hide his head un - der his wing, poor thing!

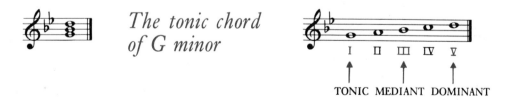

The tonic chord of G minor

TONIC   MEDIANT   DOMINANT

31

JESU, JOY OF MAN'S DESIRING

Words by Robert Bridges

This CHORALE (hymn) was composed by Johann Shop. In the arrangement for choir and orchestra by J. S. Bach (Cantata No. 147) the important part for oboe is known as an obbligato.

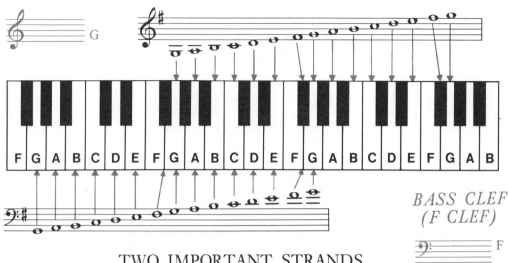

TWO IMPORTANT STRANDS
FROM BACH'S TEXTURE

(THE MELODY AND THE BASS)

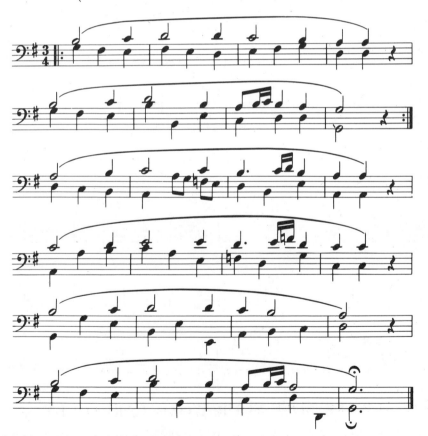

They are played on the recording by horn and bassoon.
Practise following the score as you listen to the performance.

Writing in the Bass Clef

Can you complete these musical sentences?

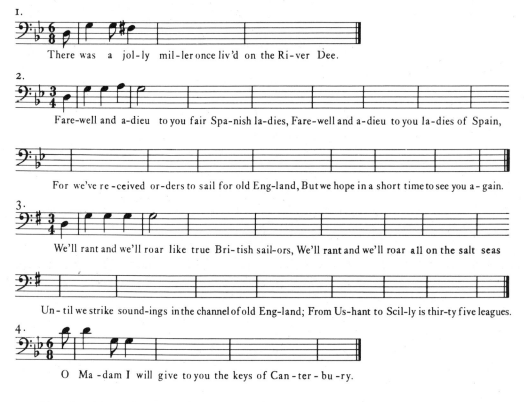

1. There was a jol-ly mil-ler once liv'd on the Ri-ver Dee.

2. Fare-well and a-dieu to you fair Spa-nish la-dies, Fare-well and a-dieu to you la-dies of Spain,

For we've re-ceived or-ders to sail for old Eng-land, But we hope in a short time to see you a-gain.

3. We'll rant and we'll roar like true Bri-tish sail-ors, We'll rant and we'll roar all on the salt seas

Un-til we strike sound-ings in the channel of old Eng-land; From Us-hant to Scil-ly is thir-ty five leagues.

4. O Ma-dam I will give to you the keys of Can-ter-bu-ry.

Give the title and composer of each of the next three examples and also name the key.

5.

6.

7.

ALWAYS EDIT YOUR WORK CAREFULLY

How many examples of S Y N C O P A T I O N can you find opposite?

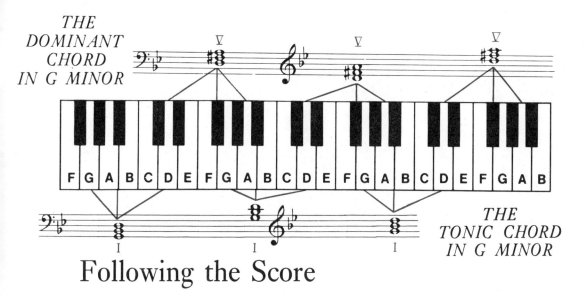

THE
DOMINANT
CHORD
IN G MINOR

THE
TONIC CHORD
IN G MINOR

Following the Score

Can you follow both treble and bass parts together?

Mozart, Symphony No. 40 in G minor

Giles Farnaby, 'Tower Hill'

TIED NOTES

A slur connecting two notes of the same pitch
indicates that the second note is not to be struck
again. How many examples can you find on this page?

Three Folk-Songs

LONG JOHN

With his shin - y blade,— Got it in his hand,—

Gon-na chop out the live oaks, That are in this land,—

He's Long John,— He's long gone,—

He's gone, gone—— Like a tur-key in the corn,—

With his long clothes on,— He's long gone,—

He's long gone,—— He's gone, He's— long— gone.—

Sing this as a response song, with a leader and a chorus, as in the early pages of Chapter One.

Mark the accents heavily to represent the axe blows of the prisoners as they cut down trees, e.g.,

Clap
Stamp

This 'blues' song is about a prisoner who escaped from the bloodhounds sent to track him down.

How many examples of TIED NOTES can you find on this page?　　*How many examples of SYNCOPATION can you find on this page?*

YANGTZE BOATMEN'S CHANTEY

Slowly and steadily

1. Ri - ver boat-men we, Toil - ing night and day,
2. Yah, hoo, yah, hoo, hay! Yah, hoo, yah, hoo, hay!

Backs bend-ing, ropes tight'ning, Sing we loud our lay.
Yai, yai, yai, hai, yai, yai, Yah, hoo, yah, hoo, hay!

A SONG FROM RUSSIA

Words translated by Rosa Newmarch

Rather quickly

S. 1 / S. 2

Oh! thou duck, dear duck of the mea - dows!

Liou - li, liou - li duck of the mea - dows!

Liou - li, duck of the mea - dows!

2. Where dost sleep when fall night's shadows?
   Liouli, liouli.

3. 'Neath the shelter of the willows.
   Liouli, liouli.

POLONAISE IN G MINOR *by J. S. Bach*

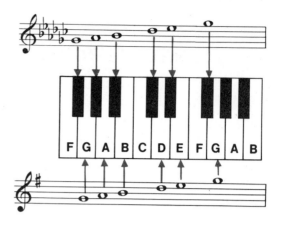

CHAPTER THREE

Pentatonic

O BY AND BY

Negro Spiritual

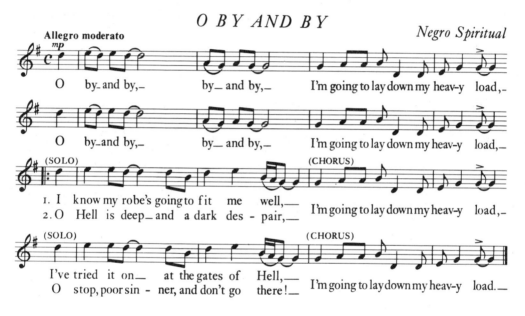

O by and by,— by and by,— I'm going to lay down my heav-y load,—

O by and by,— by and by,— I'm going to lay down my heav-y load,—

(SOLO) (CHORUS)

1. I know my robe's going to fit me well,— I'm going to lay down my heav-y load,—
2. O Hell is deep and a dark des-pair,—

(SOLO) (CHORUS)

I've tried it on— at the gates of Hell,— I'm going to lay down my heav-y load.—
O stop, poor sin-ner, and don't go there!—

THE THRUSH

Zoltán Kodály
(1882–1967)

Sings the thrush; Hark! how he war-bles

In the for-est, in the mea-dow, in the for-est,

o-ver-head. "Lis-ten to my voice", Sings the thrush. Sings the thrush.

in the mea-dow, in the for-est, in the mea-dow, sings the thrush.

REVEILLE

Zoltán Kodály

Tra, la, la! At dawn we jump a-stride the wait-ing sad-dle, Tra, la, la!

Tra, la, la, la! Tra, la, la, la, la! The bu-gle starts a stir-ring tune. Get you up, no time to waste, the

la! The bu-gle blows! Get you up, no time to waste, The coun-try-side's in-vi-ting you. Tra, la, la! The morn-ing Sun is ri-ding too.

bu-gle blows! Tra, la, la, la! The sun is ri-ding too.

THE RETURNED SAILOR

Norfolk Folk-Song

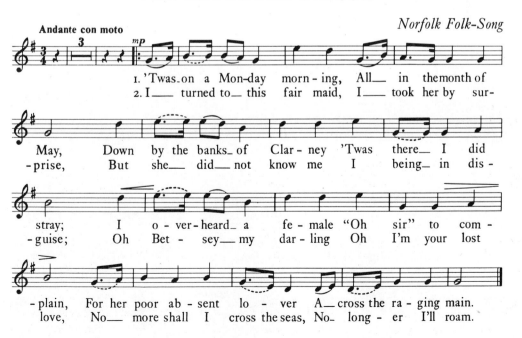

1. 'Twas on a Mon-day morn-ing, All in the month of May, Down by the banks of Clar-ney 'Twas there I did stray; I o-ver-heard a fe-male "Oh sir" to com-plain, For her poor ab-sent lo-ver A-cross the ra-ging main.

2. I turned to this fair maid, I took her by sur-prise, But she did not know me I being in dis-guise; Oh Bet-sey my dar-ling Oh I'm your lost love, No more shall I cross the seas, No long-er I'll roam.

A Song from the Hebrides

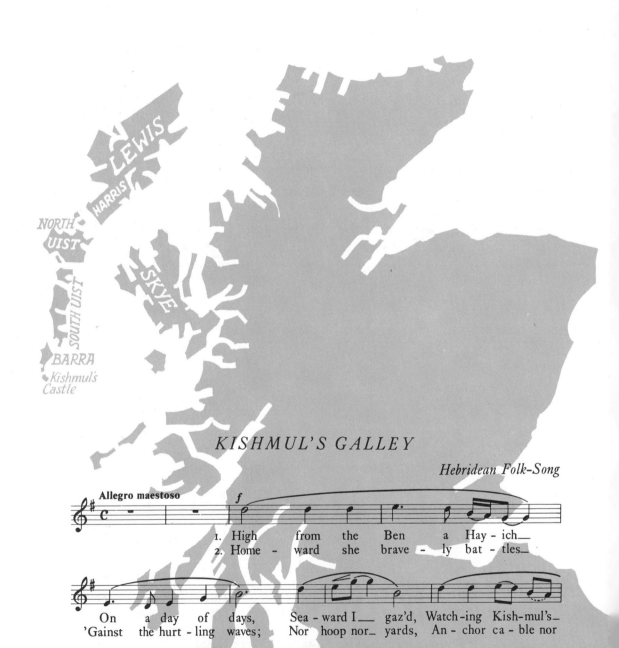

KISHMUL'S GALLEY

Hebridean Folk-Song

Allegro maestoso

1. High from the Ben a Hay - ich__
2. Home - ward she brave - ly bat - tles__

On a day of days, Sea - ward I__ gaz'd, Watch - ing Kish - mul's__
'Gainst the hurt - ling waves; Nor hoop nor__ yards, An - chor ca - ble nor

ben legato

gal - ley sail - ing.__ O - hi - o, hu - o,__ fal - u - o.
tack - le has she.__ O - hi - o, hu - o,__ fal - u - o.

40

THE STAR OF THE COUNTY DOWN

Irish Folk-Song

Words by Cathal MacGarvey

Moderato

1. Near to Ban-bridge town, in the Coun-ty Down On a morn-ing in Ju-ly, Down a bo-reen green came a sweet col-leen And she smiled as she passed me by, Oh! she looked so neat, from her two white feet To the sheen of her nut-brown hair, Such a coax-in' elf, I'd to shake my-self, To make sure I was real-ly there. Oh! from

CHORUS

Ban-try Bay up to Der-ry Quay, And from Gal-way to Dub-lin town, No maid I've seen like the brown col-leen that I met in the Coun-ty Down.

2. As she onward sped I scratch'd my head
And I gazed with a feelin' quare,
There I said, says I, to a passer by
'Who's the maid with the nut-brown hair?'
Oh! he smiled at me, and with pride says he,
'That's the gem of Ireland's crown,
Young Rosie McCann, from the banks of the Bann,
She's the star of the County Down.'

3. At the Harvest Fair she'll be surely there,
So I'll dress in my Sunday clothes,
And I'll try sheep's eyes and deludtherin lies,
On the heart of the nut-brown Rose.
No pipe I'll smoke, no horse I'll yoke,
Tho' my plough with rust turn brown,
Till a smiling bride by my own fire-side,
Sits the star of the County Down.

Chorus:
From Bantry Bay up to Derry Quay,
And from Galway to Dublin town,
No maid I've seen like the brown colleen
That I met in the County Down.

Composing

A FARMER WENT TROTTING

Words anon.

A raven cried 'Croak' and they all tumbled down,
   Bumpety, bumpety, bump!
The mare broke her knees and the farmer his
   crown,
   Lumpety, lumpety, lump!

The mischievous raven flew laughing away,
   Bumpety, bumpety, bump!
And said he would serve them the same the next
   day,
   Lumpety, lumpety, lump!

THE FERRYMAN

Words by Christina Rossetti

NICHOLAS NYE

Words by Walter de la Mare

Sadly

mf

Ni-cho-las Nye was lean and grey,

p

Poor Ni-cho-las Nye,—

Lame of a leg and old,—

Poor Ni-cho-las Nye,—

More than a score of don - key's years He had

Poor Ni-cho-las Nye,—

seen since he was foaled;—

He

He munched the this-tles, pur-ple and spiked,

munched the this-tles, pur-ple and spiked, would some-times stoop and sigh,—

munched the this-tles pur-ple and spiked, would some-times stoop and sigh,—

sigh,— sigh,— and turn his head, as if he said,

sigh,— sigh,— and turn his head, as if he said, 'Poor Ni-cho-las

'Poor Ni-cho-las, Poor Ni-cho-las, Poor ___ Ni-cho-las Nye!'

'Poor Ni-cho-las, Poor Ni-cho-las, Poor ___ Ni-cho-las Nye!'

VIVE L'EAU!

Vive l'eau! Vive l'eau!
Qui rafraîchit et rend propre.
Vive l'eau! Vive l'eau!
Qui nous lave et nous rend beaux.

1. C'est sa fraîcheur qui nous donne
   La vigueur et la santé.
   Et le bon Dieu nous ordonne
   D'aimer bien la propreté.
      Vive l'eau, etc.

2. Tout petit enfant bien sage
   Doit se laver tous les jours
   Les mains, le corps, le visage,
   Pour se faire aimer toujours.
      Vive l'eau, etc.

3. C'est l'eau qui nous désaltère
   Et cuit tous nos aliments.
   En pluie, en vapeur légère,
   Elle féconde nos champs.
      Vive l'eau, etc.

4. Elle retombe en resée
   Sur les fleurs tous les matins,
   Et par l'homme utilisée,
   Fait tourner de gais moulins.
      Vive l'eau, etc.

CHORUS

Vi - ve l'eau! Vi - ve l'eau! Qui ra - fraî-chit et rend pro - pre.

Vi - ve l'eau! Vi - ve l'eau! Qui nous lave et nous rend beaux. *Fin*

VERSE

1.C'est sa fraî - cheur qui nous don - ne La vi - gueur et la san - té.

Et le bon Dieu nous or - don - ne D'aim-er bien la pro - pre-té.

Hurrah for Water! Hurrah for Water!
Which refreshes and cleanses.
Hurrah for Water! Hurrah for Water!
Which washes and beautifies us.

Its freshness gives us
Vigour and health.
And the good Lord commands us
To cherish cleanliness.

Every well-behaved child
Must wash himself daily,
His hands, his body, his face,
So that he may always be loved.

Water quenches our thirst
And cooks all our food.
As rain, as light mist,
It fertilises our fields.

It falls as dew
On the flowers each morning,
And is used by man
To turn his gay mills.

DANCE FOR THE BLACK KEYS

Zoltán Kodály

Shapes and Patterns

Notice how the artist, like the composer, explores the ways in which his scraps of material may be assembled to produce interesting wholes.

Music Workshop

IDEAS FOR PATTERNS

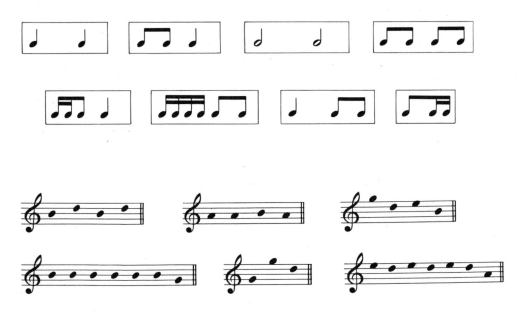

Composing

STORMALONG

Words anon.

Old Stor- my he is dead and gone, To my way, To my way, Storm-a - long!

To my way,———— Storm - a-long!

1. Old Stormy he is dead and gone,
   To my way, Stormalong!
   Old Stormy he is dead and gone,
   Aye, aye, aye, Mister Stormalong.

2. Old Stormy's dead, that good old man,
   To my way, Stormalong!
   Old Stormy's dead, that good old man,
   Aye, aye, aye, Mister Stormalong.

3. I carried him away to Mobile Bay,

4. I dug his grave with a silver spade,

5. I lowered him down with a golden chain,

6. I dug his grave full wide and deep,

7. I wish I was Old Stormy's son,

8. Old Stormy he is dead and gone.

THE CAT

Words by W. H. Davies

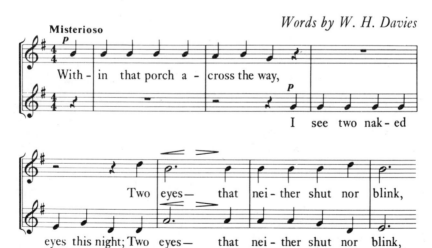

With - in that porch a - cross the way,

I see two nak- ed

Two eyes— that nei - ther shut nor blink,

eyes this night; Two eyes— that nei - ther shut nor blink,

Within that porch across the way,
  I see two naked eyes this night;
Two eyes that neither shut nor blink,
  Searching my face with a green light.

But cats to me are strange, so strange—
  I cannot sleep if one is near;
And though I'm sure I see those eyes,
  I'm not so sure a body's there!

THE TWO RATS

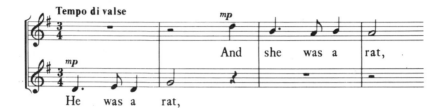

He was a rat, and she was a rat,
  And down in one hole they did dwell,
And both were as black as a witch's cat,
  And they loved one another well.

He had a tail, and she had a tail,
  Both long and curling and fine;
And each said, 'Yours is the finest tail
  In the world excepting mine'.

Anon.

THE TIDY WIFE

I married my wife by the light of the moon,
  A tidy housewife,* a tidy one;
She never gets up until it is noon,
  And I hope she'll prove a tidy one.

And when she gets up, she makes such haste,
  A tidy housewife, a tidy one;
She takes up the poker to roll out the paste,
  And I hope she'll prove a tidy one.

*(pronounced 'huzzif')

Anon.

SNORING AT SEA

On deck beneath the awning,
I dozing lay and yawning;
It was the grey of dawning,
  Ere yet the sun arose.

And above the funnel's roaring,
And the fitful wind's deploring,
I heard the cabin snoring
  With universal nose.

W. M. Thackeray

THE SMUGGLERS

O my true love's a smuggler and sails upon the
  sea,
And I would I were a seaman to go along with he;
To go along with he for the satins and the wine,
And run the tubs at Slapton when the stars do
  shine.

Anon.

AUX QUATRE COINS DE PARIS

1. Aux quatre coins de Paris
   Devinez ce qu'il y a?
   Il y a un bois,
   Un petit bois joli, Mesdames,
   Il y a un bois,
   Un petit bois joli il y'a.

2. Et dedans ce petit bois,
   Devinez ce qu'il y a?
   Il y a un arbre joli, Mesdames,
   Il y a un arbre,
   Un petit arbre joli il y'a.

3. Et dessus ce petit arbre,
   Devinez ce qu'il y a?
   Il y a un nid, etc.

4. Et dedans ce petit nid,
   Devinez ce qu'il y a?
   Il y a un oeuf, etc.

5. Et dedans ce petit oeuf,
   Devinez ce qu'il y a?
   Il y a un blanc, etc.

6. Et dedans ce petit blanc,
   Devinez ce qu'il y a?
   Il y a un jaune, etc.

7. Et dedans ce petit jaune,
   Devinez ce qu'il y a?
   Il y a écrit:
   Vot' petit serviteur, Mesdames,
   Vot' petit serviteur je suis.

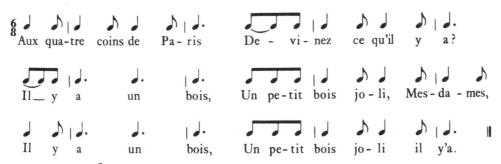

Aux qua-tre coins de Pa- ris De - vi- nez ce qu'il y a?

Il_ y a un bois, Un pe-tit bois jo-li, Mes-da - mes,

Il y a un bois, Un pe-tit bois jo- li il y'a.

DANCE FOR THE BLACK KEYS
Zoltán Kodály

53

CHAPTER FOUR

The Dominant Seventh (V⁷)

THE MANGO WALK

Jamaican Folk-Song

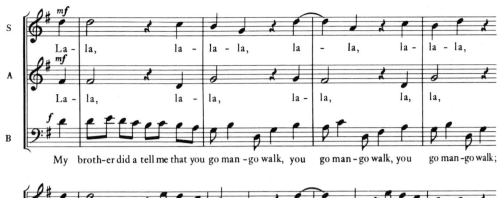

S: La-la, la - la-la, la - la, la-la-la,

A: La-la, la - la, la - la, la, la,

B: My broth-er did a tell me that you go man-go walk, you go man-go walk, you go man-go walk;

S: la - la, la-la-la- la - la, la - la, la-la-la-la - la.

A: la - la, la-la-la -la, la - la, la-la-la- la - la.

B: My broth-er did a tell me that you go man- go walk and steal all the num - ber 'lev - en.

S A: I tell you Sue, I tell you for true, I tell you for true, I tell you

B: I tell you Sue, I tell you for true, I tell you for true, I tell you

S A: That I don't go to no man - go walk and steal all the num - ber 'lev-en.

B: That I don't go to no man - go walk and steal all the num - ber 'lev-en.

How many times can you find this bar in 'The Mango Walk'?

These four notes form the DOMINANT SEVENTH—

Root Third Fifth Seventh V⁷

The seventh makes a discord with the Root. It resolves by falling a step:

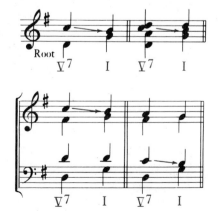

55

SKIP TO MY LOU

Traditional party song

Lightly

Chorus Skip, skip, skip to my Lou, Skip, skip, skip to my Lou,

Skip, skip, skip to my Lou, Skip to my Lou, my dar - ling.

1. Lost my part-ner, what'll I do? Lost my part-ner what'll I do?

Lost my part-ner, what'll I do? Skip to my Lou my dar - ling.

2. I'll hitch a-noth-er one a bet-ter one too, I'll hitch a-noth-er one a bet-ter one too,

I'll hitch a-noth-er one a bet-ter one too, Skip to my Lou my dar - ling.

3. Pa's got a shot-gun, Num-ber thir-ty-two, Pa's got a shot-gun, Num-ber thir-ty-two,

Pa's got a shot-gun, Num-ber thir-ty-two, Skip to my Lou my dar - ling.

56

In verse 1 the bass includes only the Root of chord I (G) and the Root of V (D).

Verse 2 includes the third of chord I (B) and all the notes of V⁷ (D, F♯, A, C).

Verse 3 includes both the third and the fifth of chord I (B, D).

In the final chorus the bass is syncopated.

SWEET ORANGE (NARANJA DULCE)

Costa Rican Folk-Song
(Translated Ruth E. Barnard)

We have suggested an Alto part for the first line. Compose an Alto part for the rest yourself.

WIEGENLIED

Franz Schubert

(1797–1828)

1. Slumber, slumber, sweet my joy and treasure
   Gently, gently, rock'd by mother's hand.
   Golden slumbers, dreams of azure,
   Hover round thee, safe in slumber land.

2. Slumber, slumber, in thy nest enfolden
   Slumber, sheltered by thy mother's arm.
   All her treasure, bright and golden,
   Mother's love now claspeth safe from harm.

3. Slumber, slumber, till thine eye uncloses,
   'Lulla, Lulla,' mother's voice will sing.
   Two white lilies, two red roses,
   When thou wakest she her babe will bring.

Tr. by Albert G. Latham

NON-HARMONY NOTES (UNESSENTIAL NOTES)

pn   a note which moves by step from one harmony note to the next harmony note is called a **passing note**.

apn a passing note sung on the beat is called an **accented passing note**.

an   a note one step above or below a harmony note and which returns to that harmony note is called an **auxiliary note**.

STREETS OF LAREDO

American Cowboy Song

2. 'I see by your outfit that you are a cowboy,'
   These words he did say as I boldly walked by;
   'Come sit down beside me and hear my sad
      story,
   I'm shot in the breast and I know I must die.

3. 'Get six jolly cowboys to carry my coffin,
   Get six purty maidens to sing me a song,
   Take me to the valley and lay the sod o'er me,
   For I'm a young cowboy and know I've done
      wrong.

4. 'Oh, beat the drum slowly and play the fife
      lowly,
   Play the dead march as you carry me along;
   Put bunches of roses all over my coffin,
   Roses to deaden the clods as they fall.'

Complete the Alto part in this song making use of passing and auxiliary notes
where appropriate.

BANANA BOAT LOADERS

Jamaican Folk-Song

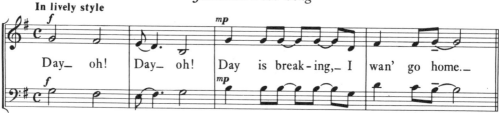

Day_ oh! Day_ oh! Day is break-ing,_ I wan' go home._

1. Come, Mis-ter Tal- ly-man come tal - ly my ba-na-nas. Day is break-ing I wan' go home._
2. Came here for work, I did-n't come here for to i-dle. Day is break-ing I wan' go home._

(shout)   (shout)

Three han', four han', five han', Bunch! Six han', seven han', eight han', Bunch!

Day is break-ing_ I wan' go home._
4. So check them and check them but
5. My back is a break - ing with
6. Don't give me all the bunches I'm no

|4 - 5 |6

check with cau - tion. Day is break-ing, I wan' go home._
bare ex - haus - tion. Day is break-ing, I wan' go home._
horse with bri - dle. Day is break-ing, I wan' go home.

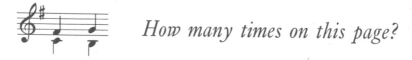

How many times on this page?

The third of the dominant is a semitone below the tonic:

The leading note is the third of the dominant seventh:

Root   3rd   5th   7th

It is known as the LEADING NOTE as it so often leads to the tonic:

I   wan'   go   home

Sounded together, the 3rd and 7th form a discord which can be resolved if each part moves a semitone in contrary motion:

Intervals

These intervals are found in the pentatonic scale:

Perfect Concords

Octaves (Perfect 8ves) Perfect 5th; Perfect 4th;   Perfect 5th; Perfect 4th; Perfect 5th; Perfect 4th;

Imperfect Concords

Major 3rd;   Minor 6th.   Major 6th;   Minor 3rd   Minor 3rd;   Major 6th.

Mild Discords

Major 2nd;   Minor 7th.   Major 2nd;   Minor 7th.   Major 2nd;   Minor 7th.

In addition to the intervals shown above, the full major scale, which includes C and F♯, involves the following

Harsh Discords

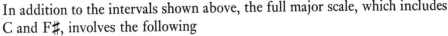

Minor 2nd;   Major 7th.   Minor 2nd;   Major 7th.   Augmented 4th; Diminished 5th.

The inversion (= upside-down form) of a *major* interval is a *minor* interval. The inversion of an *augmented* interval is a *diminished* interval

Point out an Augmented 4th in 'Banana Boat Loaders'
a Diminished 5th in 'Streets of Laredo'
a Minor 7th in 'Wiegenlied'
a Major 2nd in 'The Mango Walk'

SLEDGING

Russian Folk-Song

Words by Frances B. Wood

Sing a song of win-try weath-er, Snow-flakes light as down-y feath-er,
Hill and field and road to-geth - er, 'Neath their man-tle hi - ding.
Hear the mer-ry laugh-ter ring-ing, Girls and boys are gai - ly sing-ing,
Glad that win-ter-time is bring-ing days to go a - slid - ing.

2. Sledges ready, off we scurry
   Clad in coats and mufflers furry;
   To the snowy hills we hurry,
   Where the drifts are lying.

3. Down the slippery slopes we're gliding
   Faster, faster onwards riding,
   Skilfully our sledges guiding,
   Past each other flying.

The notes of the dominant and dominant seventh chords are the same in the minor mode as in the major:

When writing in the minor mode we have to indicate the sharp before the F as an *accidental* because it does not occur in the Key signature. In the minor mode the dominant seventh resolves by falling a *tone*—

Point out in 'Sledging'

1 an example of the dominant chord with F♯ as the lowest note:

2 an example of the dominant seventh chord with F♯ as the lowest note:

3 an example of the dominant seventh chord with A as the lowest note and the F♯ omitted:

4 an example of the dominant chord with the root D as the lowest note:

5 all the examples of the tonic chord. How many times does it occur?

The tonic chord of G minor is sustained throughout bars 1 and 2 yet the Solo part includes a note that does not belong to the chord. It would be possible to change the chord to V for this quaver:

but this would produce a fussy or jerky effect out of keeping with the style of the song. The A then, is treated as a 'non-harmony note' which passes by step between two harmony notes and is called a *passing note*.
Name the passing notes in bars 4, 6, 10, 12, and 14.

THE MARCH OF THE THREE KINGS

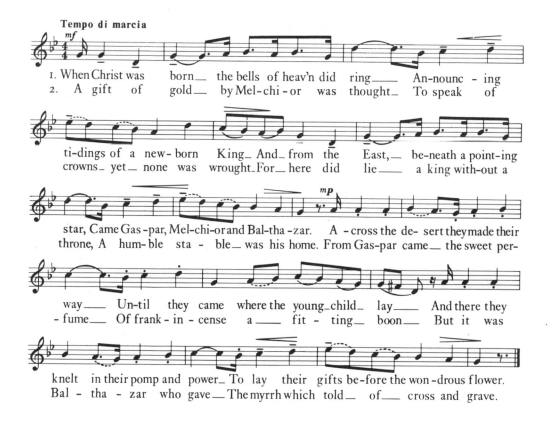

Tempo di marcia

1. When Christ was born_ the bells of heav'n did ring___ An-nounc - ing
2. A gift of gold_ by Mel-chi - or was thought_ To speak of

ti-dings of a new- born King_ And_ from the East,_ be-neath a point-ing
crowns_ yet_ none was wrought_For_ here did lie___ a king with-out a

star, Came Gas -par, Mel-chi-or and Bal-tha -zar. A - cross the de- sert they made their
throne, A hum- ble sta - ble_ was his home. From Gas-par came_ the sweet per-

way___ Un-til they came where the young_child_ lay___ And there they
- fume_ Of frank - in - cense a ___ fit - ting_ boon_ But it was

knelt in their pomp and power_ To lay their gifts be-fore the won -drous flower.
Bal - tha - zar who gave_ The myrrh which told_ of_ cross and grave.

This Christmas tune comes from Provence, as does the Farandole which
follows. Both tunes are used by Bizet in the music he wrote for a play
called *L'Arlésienne*. The Farandole is a quick dance in which the tambourine
figures prominently. You might choose to play it before and after the singing
to suggest the arrival and departure of the kings and their retinue.

FARANDOLE

65

O MA TENDRE MUSETTE

This is an eighteenth-century *Bergerette* (i.e. a shepherd's song, or a piece in a simple, pastoral style). The music is by Monsigny, arranged by J. B. Weckerlin.

The *musette* is a member of the bagpipe family and was very popular in France during the reigns of Louis XIV and Louis XV. The song that follows is typical of the kind of tune that was played on the musette. Notice that the piano accompaniment suggests the drone of the bagpipe and gives an impression of the grace notes and rapid passages with which these eighteenth-century pastoral airs were embellished.

O ma ten-dre mu-set - te, Con-so-le ma dou-leur;—

Par - le moi de Li-set - te, Ce nom fait mon bon - heur.—

Je la re-vois plus bel - le, Plus bel-le tous les jours—

Je me plains tou-jours d'el - le, Et je l'ai-me tou - jours!—

A Lullaby from Norway

In 1893 Edvard Grieg spent a holiday in the Norwegian mountains in the company of his Dutch friend, Julius Röntgen. The following quotation is from one of Röntgen's letters:

'In Skogadalsboe we had an unforgettable evening. At that time the tourist hut was in charge of Tollef and Brit Holmstad. The wife had recently had a child and her sister, Gjendine Slaalien, was staying with her to help her. This Gjendine, born near the Gjendin lake, had been named after it by her parents. She was the only person in Norway with this name. When we first saw her she was rocking her sister's child in her arms, singing it to sleep with the following song:'

GJENDINE'S LULLABY

Words translated by John Horton

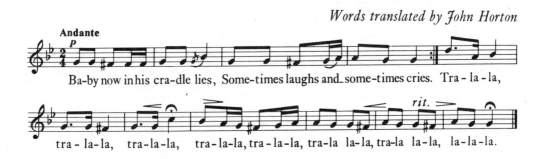

Ba-by now in his cra-dle lies, Some-times laughs and some-times cries. Tra - la la,

tra - la-la, tra-la-la, tra - la-la, tra - la-la, tra - la la-la, tra - la la-la, la-la-la.

TUTU MARAMBA

Brazilian Folk-Song

Words by Julia W. Bingham

Tu - tu Ma - ram - ba, ___ stop scratch-ing at my door.___

The mas - ter is home, He will fright-en you a - way.___

Tu - tu Ma - ram - ba, ___ don't come here an - y more; ___

My child must be safe in his sleep, in his play.___

Loud-ly ring-ing bells will drive a - way all e - vil things,

Things that lurk in dusk - y holes or dart on cru - el wings.___

A - ran - ha Ta - tan - ha, A - ran - ha Ta - tan - ha,

If Tu - tu should come back, he must sure - ly find you sleep - ing.

A - ran - ha Ta - tan - ha, A - ran - ha Ta - tan - ha,

All night by your bed I my watch will be keep - ing.

Soft - ly sound the ev -'ning bells that mark the com - ing night;

Na - ture sinks to peace - ful rest un - til the morn - ing light.___

Tu - tu Ma - ram - ba____ stop scratch-ing at my door.____

The mas - ter is home, He will fright-en you a - way.____

Tu - tu Ma-ram- ba____ don't come here an - y more.____

My child must be safe in his sleep, in his play.____

(Tutu Maramba is a bogyman in Brazilian folk lore.)

Notice the treatment of the word 'evil'. F sharp is followed by E flat. This produces an *augmented interval* and a strained effect. Practice carefully until you can sing this passage accurately and expressively.

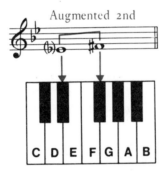

Augmented 2nd

In the next line the more usual major second is used:

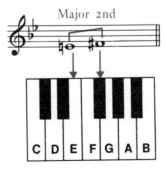

Major 2nd

Find another example of an augmented second.

Things to Do

Compose a tune for the following poem. Use the scale of G minor and experiment with the interval of the augmented second to suggest a sad and wintry atmosphere.

THE FISHER'S WIDOW

1. The boats go out and the boats come in
   Under the wintry sky;
   And the rain and foam are white in the wind,
   And the white gulls cry.

2. She sees the sea, when the wind is wild,
   Swept by the windy rain;
   And her heart's a-weary of sea and land
   As the long days wane.

3. She sees the torn sails fly in the foam,
   Broad on the sky-line grey;
   And the boats go out and the boats come in,
   But there's one away.

Arthur Symons

ALOUETTE

French-Canadian Folk-Song

A - lou-et - te, gen-tille A-lou-et - te, A - lou-et - te, Je te plu-me-rai.

1. Je te plu-me-rai la tête, Je te plu-me-rai la tête, {Et la tête, Et la tête, A-lou-ette, A-lou-ette} Oh!

2. Je te plu-me-rai le bec, Je te plu-me-rai le bec. {Et le bec, Et le bec, Et la tête, Et la tete, A-lou-ette, A-lou-ette,} Oh!

3. Le nez (nose)   4. Le dos (back)   5. Les pattes (claws)   6. Le cou (neck).

Complete the bass part.

CHAPTER FIVE

Related Keys

THE INSTRUMENT SONG

Willi Geisler

Ländler tempo

Now first comes the o - boe so pun - gent and bit - ing,

Its pas - tor - al e - choes our sen - ses de - light - ing,

And next comes the flute, with ea - sy flow;

The mu - sic rocks gen - tly to and fro.

The horn has on - ly one note to play,

It makes a cre - scen - do, then dies a - way.

The clar - in - et plays smooth - ly and sweet - ly,

It ri - ses and falls, does ev - 'ry - thing neat - ly.

The deep bas - soon then takes its place;

With mea - sured tread sup - plies the bass.

B♭ major is the relative major of G minor

The tonic chord of
B♭ major
B♭ : I

The dominant seventh
of B♭ major
B♭ : V7

Three Songs from Russia

ON THE BANK

Words by Jacqueline Froom

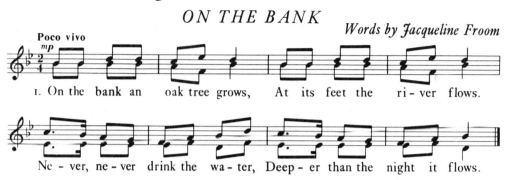

Poco vivo
mp

1. On the bank an oak tree grows, At its feet the ri-ver flows.

Ne-ver, ne-ver drink the wa-ter, Deep-er than the night it flows.

2. On the bank a birch tree grows,
At its feet the river flows.
Never, never drink the water,
Faster than the wind it flows.

3. Where the birch and oak trees grow
Deep and dark the waters flow.
Never, never drink the waters,
Colder than the dead they flow.

A RUSSIAN CRADLE SONG

Andante
P

1. Sleep my darl - ing, sleep my own one,

Sleep till day is— nigh;————

While the win - ter— sleeps a - round you,

Dark———— and— still the sky.————

2. Soft the snow, it falls so gently,
Sleep till day is nigh;
Soft the wind, it only whispers,
Breathes a gentle sigh.

3. Fear no danger, little Cossack,
Sleep till day is nigh;
Though they howl, no wolves can hurt you,
Father rides nearby.

4. Brave his heart, our gallant horseman,
Sleep till day is nigh;
While he watches, strong and handsome,
Safe from harm we lie.

'A Russian Cradle Song' is based upon four chords. Can you say which bars use:

1. *the tonic chord of G minor (g: I)*
2. *the dominant chord of G minor (g: V)*
3. *the tonic chord of Bb major (Bb: I)*
4. *the dominant chord of Bb major (Bb: V)?*

THE BIRCH TREE

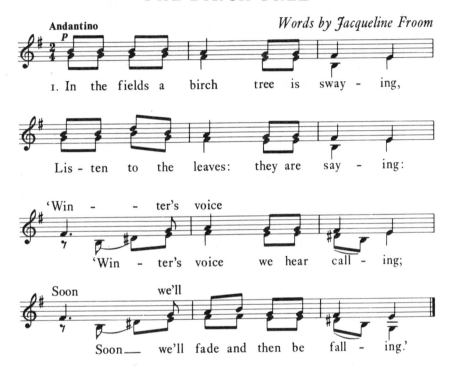

Words by Jacqueline Froom

1. In the fields a birch tree is sway - ing,
Lis - ten to the leaves: they are say - ing:
'Win - - ter's voice
'Win - ter's voice we hear call - ing;
Soon we'll
Soon___ we'll fade and then be fall - ing.'

The tonic chord of
E minor

e: I

2. In the fields a birch tree is swaying,
Listen to the branches: they are saying:
'Winter's gusts fiercely shake us,
Snowy burdens nearly break us.'

3. In the fields a birch tree is swaying,
Listen to the catkins: they are saying:
'Dance with us in the breezes
While the winter earth unfreezes.'

The dominant chord
of E minor

e: V

You will hear this folk tune in the last movement of Symphony No. 4 by Tchaikovsky.

E minor is the relative minor of G major.

GYPSY RONDO

from Piano Trio No. 1 in G by Joseph Haydn

(2nd Time—R.H. an octave lower)

GIPSY RONDO by *Joseph Haydn* (1732–1809)

A   B   A   C   A

A always begins in the   TONIC KEY   (G major)
B is in the   TONIC MINOR (G minor)
C is in the   TONIC MINOR (G minor)
and its   RELATIVE MAJOR (B♭ major)

MODULATING SEQUENCES

In bars 4–6 the same pattern of melody is repeated a tone higher.

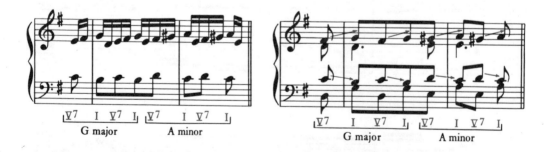

G♯ is the Leading Note in A minor.
Are the intervals in the L.H. part exactly the same?
Which are the non-harmony notes in the R.H. part?

80

Another modulating sequence occurs in bars 16-18:

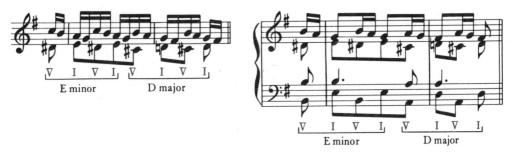

This time the pattern is repeated a step lower.

D♯ is the leading note in E minor. (E minor is the Relative Minor of G major).

C♯ is the leading note in D major. (D major is the Dominant Major of G.)

Are the intervals in the R.H. part exactly the same in each limb of the sequence?

Which are the non-harmony notes in the R.H. part?

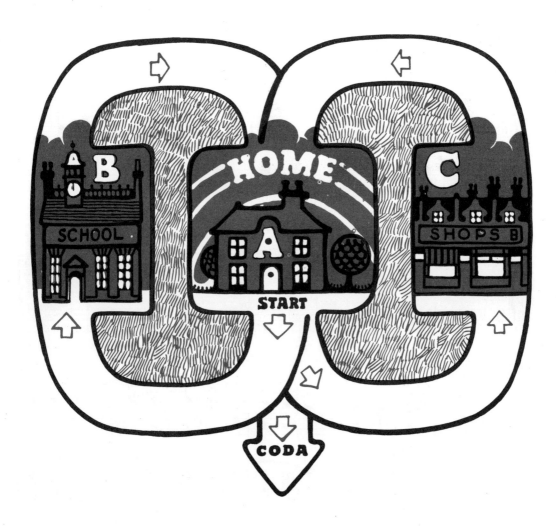

SLAVONIC DANCE

Op. 46, No. 8 by Antonín Dvořák (1841–1904)

83

85

Composer's Workshop

Now that you are familiar with the sound of Dvořák's Slavonic Dance let us examine it more closely to see what it can teach us about the way in which a composer works. Here is Dvořák's opening tune:

It contains certain basic melodic shapes and rhythmic patterns:

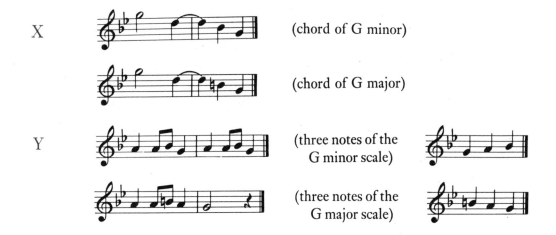

X   (chord of G minor)

               (chord of G major)

Y   (three notes of the G minor scale)

               (three notes of the G major scale)

RHYTHMIC PATTERNS

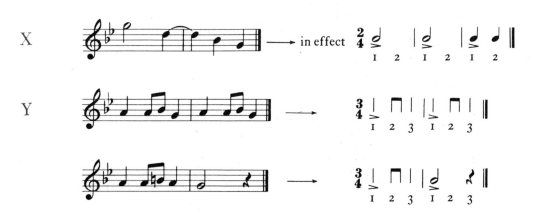

X   → in effect

Y

CONTRASTING ELEMENTS

1. TONALITY : Alternation of Minor and Major
2. RHYTHM   : Alternation of 2- and 3-beat patterns
3. DYNAMICS: Alternation of loud (ff) and soft (p)
4. PHRASING : Alternation of staccato and legato
5. MOOD   : Alternation of the striding vigour of X (the melody moves by leap) and the tripping jauntiness of Y (the melody moves mainly by step and contains some repeated notes)

SOME TRANSFORMATIONS OF X

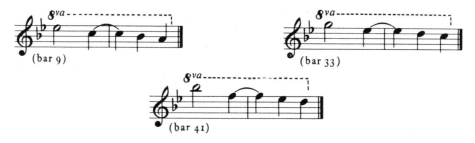

One of the most striking transformations of X occurs in the tune that marks the beginning of the middle section of the dance:

SOME TRANSFORMATIONS OF Y

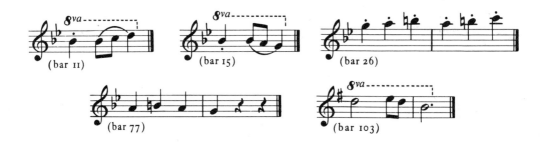

SOME COMBINATIONS OF X AND Y

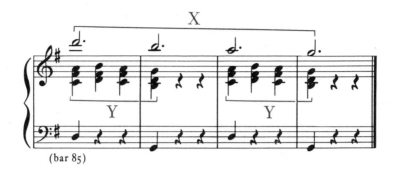

(bar 85)

You will have discovered already how superbly Dvořák has arranged his shapes and patterns. The whole piece grows from the seeds contained in the first eight bars; one melody flows naturally from another, the various sections are related and even the tiniest detail has point and musical meaning and contributes to the unity of the whole.

STRUCTURE OF THE DANCE

A	B	A	CODA
bars 1–84	bars 85–127	bars 128–199	bars 200–276
key	key	key	key
centres	centre	centres	centres
G minor;	G major	G minor;	G minor;
G major;		G major;	A minor;
B♭ major.		B♭ major.	G major.

THINGS TO DO

In which bars do we find transformations of X and combinations of X and Y other than those already listed?

In which bars does X appear in the bass?

Where do we find a tune which begins with an eight-bar pentatonic phrase? (Play this tune on your recorder and make an arrangement for two recorders.)

Find an eight-bar phrase which consists of chords V^7–I repeated four times in G major.

Look through the Coda and say which eight bars are in the key of A minor.

Dvořák wrote sixteen Slavonic Dances for piano duet and these are published in four books. Explore them and perform some of them. Find out more about Dvořák and his music and prepare a short illustrated talk that you might give to members of your class or to your school music society.

SHEPHERD'S HEY

'Shepherd's Hey' is a Morris Dance tune which was noted down by Cecil Sharp in 1906 from the playing of the Bidford Morris Dancers (J. Mason, Stow on the Wold; W. Hathaway, Cheltenham; and William Wells, Bampton). In 1913 Percy Grainger made his well-known arrangement for piano and this is referred to in the present setting which is scored for oboe, clarinet, violin, violoncello and piano.

In our arrangement we introduce the tunes which are printed below. They do not occur in the order in which they are printed. Try to hear these tunes in your mind and then sing them a number of times, making sure that you are familiar with them before listening to the recording.

1. Note down the order in which the tunes occur. (A, B, C, etc.)
2. Identify the instrument which plays each tune on its first appearance.
3. There is a short passage in G minor (the *tonic* minor). What are the string players doing at this point? Name the tune which follows immediately after this passage as the music moves back to G major.
4. There is a passage in E minor (the *relative* minor). Which two tunes occur in this section?
5. Towards the end of the piece you will hear a well-known tune X which is not included below. Can you identify it?

Fire down below

A

The Volga Boat Song

B

The Keel Row

C

Ballet ('Petite Suite', Debussy)

On with the motley ('I Pagliacci', Leoncavallo)

Can-Can ('Orpheus in the Underworld', Offenbach)

There's nae luck about the house

The blue bells of Scotland

Pentatonic Jigsaw

Piece together the tunes and discover a number sequence.

Acknowledgements are due to the following for permission to reproduce extracts from poems, songs, or music: Anglo-Soviet Music Press Ltd. (Kabalevsky's 'A Little Joke' from *Fifteen Children's Pieces*); Boosey & Hawkes Ltd. (Kodály's 'The Thrush' and 'Reveille' from *Bicinia Hungarica* Book I, Kodály's 'Dance for the Black Keys' from *Children's Dances* for piano, 'The Star of the County Down' from *Irish Country Songs* Vol. IV edited and arranged by Herbert Hughes, and Kennedy-Fraser's 'Kishmul's Galley' from *Songs of the Hebrides* Volume I); Jonathan Cape Ltd. ('The Cat' from *The Complete Poems of W. H. Davies*); J. & W. Chester Ltd. ('Duck of the Meadows' from *Russian Folk-Songs*, selected and translated by Rosa Newmarch); Cooperative Recreation Service, Inc. ('Yangtze Boatmen's Chantey' from *The Pagoda—Thirteen Chinese Songs*); J. Curwen & Sons Ltd. (Warlock's 'Mattachins' from *Capriol Suite*); Dodd, Mead & Co. Inc. and William Heinemann Ltd. ('The Fisher's Widow' from *The Poems of Arthur Symons*); Mrs. Marjory Kennedy-Fraser's Trust ('Kishmul's Galley' from *Songs of the Hebrides* Volume I); Leeds Music Corporation (Kabalevsky's 'A Little Joke' from *Fifteen Children's Pieces*); Modern Language Association of America ('Sweet Orange' ('Naranja Dulce') from *Beginning Spanish in Grade Three* Appendix I, edited by Mary P. Thompson et al.); Novello & Co. Ltd. ('The Keys of Canterbury' from *Collected Folk Songs* Book I and *Shepherd's Hey*, Morris Dance Tune collected by Cecil Sharp and Herbert C. MacIlwaine); Silver Burdett Company (the words of 'Tutu Maramba' from *Music Around the World*); The Literary Trustees of Walter de la Mare and the Society of Authors as their representative (de la Mare's *Nicholas Nye*); Wesleyan University Press ('The Cat' from *The Complete Poems of W. H. Davies*); Oxford University Press (the translation of 'Wiegenlied' from *Clarendon Song Books* Book I, 'Banana Boat Loaders' from *Folk-Songs of Jamaica*, the translation by John Horton of 'Gjendine's Lullaby' from *Scenes from Scandinavia*, Robert Bridges's words to Bach's *Jesu, Joy of Man's Desiring*, the words of 'On the Bank' and 'Birch Tree' from *Children's Songs of Russia*, the words of 'Sledging' from *A Second Sixty Songs for Little Children*; Voggenreiter Verlag ('The Instrument Song'); Schott & Co. Ltd. (Percy Grainger's arrangement of *Shepherd's Hey*).

First published 1968
Reprinted 1968

Engraved and printed in Holland by
N.V. Gebr. Keesmaat, Haarlem